ICONS

BAHIA STYLE

BAHIA

Exteriors   Interiors

STYLE

Details

PHOTOS **Tuca Reinés**
EDITOR **Angelika Taschen**

TASCHEN

HONG KONG KÖLN LONDON LOS ANGELES MADRID PARIS TOKYO

Front cover: Wonderful sea views: from the veranda of Fazenda Calá on the coast of Barra do Prateaçu.
Couverture: Une vue imprenable : de la véranda de la Fazenda Calá on voit la mer devant Barra do Prateaçu.
Umschlagvorderseite: Beste Aussichten: Von der Veranda der Fazenda Calá blickt man aufs Meer vor Barra do Prateaçu.

Back cover: Welcome to Brazil: the keyring is designed like the country's flag.
Dos de couverture: Bienvenue : le porte-clés évoque les formes et les couleurs du drapeau brésilien.
Umschlagrückseite: Herzlich willkommen: Der Schlüsselanhänger ist wie die Nationalflagge Brasiliens gestaltet.

Also available from TASCHEN:

Living in Bahia
Hardcover, 26 x 30.2 cm, 200 pages
ISBN 978-3-8365-0478-2 (Edition with English and German cover)
ISBN 978-3-8365-0480-5 (Edition with French cover)

To stay informed about upcoming TASCHEN titles, please request our magazine at
www.taschen.com/magazine or write to TASCHEN, Hohenzollernring 53, D-50672 Cologne,
Germany; contact@taschen.com; Fax: +49-221-254919. We will be happy to send you
a free copy of our magazine, which is filled with information about all of our books.

© 2009 TASCHEN GmbH
Hohenzollernring 53, D-50672 Köln
www.taschen.com

Concept, layout and editing by Angelika Taschen, Berlin
General project management by Stephanie Paas, Cologne
Texts by Christiane Reiter, Hamburg
English translation by John Sykes, Cologne
French translation by Michèle Schreyer, Cologne
Lithography by Thomas Grell, Cologne

Printed in China
ISBN 978-3-8365-1509-2

CONTENTS SOMMAIRE INHALT

06
THE HEART OF BRAZIL
Le cœur du Brésil   Das Herz Brasiliens

08
EXTERIORS
Extérieurs   Aussichten

72
INTERIORS
Intérieurs   Einsichten

154
DETAILS
Détails   Details

The history of Brazil began in Bahia: in 1500 the picture-perfect beach of Espelho das Maravilhas is said to have been the first land sighted by the Portuguese navigator and explorer Pedro Álvares Cabral; and in 1549 Salvador became the first capital of Brazil. The Portuguese were followed by the British and French, who forced the native Indios to work as slaves in the sugar-cane fields. Later the colonial rulers brought Africans to Bahia. These foreign powers did not stay long in the region, but they left a lasting legacy: Portuguese, Indian and African culture form a harmonious trio that shapes the attitude to life, architecture and art in Bahia to this day. The people of this federal state, which covers about 561,000 square kilometres in the north-east of Brazil, lead a relaxed and easy-going lifestyle, and love the Portuguese-influenced "tropical Baroque" style and brightly coloured accessories. The setting for Bahia's style is a breathtaking natural environment of

THE HEART OF BRAZIL

C'est ici dans l'État de Bahia que commence l'histoire du Brésil : en 1500, la superbe plage Espelho das Maravilhas aurait été la première terre aperçue par le navigateur et explorateur Pedro Álvares Cabral ; et Salvador devint en 1549 la première capitale du Brésil. Les Portugais débarquèrent, suivis des Britanniques et des Français. Les Indiens doivent alors travailler comme esclaves dans les champs de canne à sucre. Plus tard les colonisateurs amèneront aussi des Africains à Bahia. Si les puissances étrangères ne sont pas restées longtemps dans la région, l'architecture et l'art de Bahia sont encore marqués par l'influence de la culture portugaise, indienne et africaine – ainsi d'ailleurs que l'art de vivre des habitants. Dans cet État qui se déploie sur 561 000 kilomètres carrés environ au nord-est du Brésil, les gens sont détendus et sereins, aiment le « baroque tropical » importé par les Portugais et la couleur partout et toujours. Le style de Bahia est mis en valeur par son splendide cadre naturel qui offre une côte Atlantique longue d'un millier

In Bahia begann die Geschichte Brasiliens: Im Jahr 1500 soll der Bilderbuchstrand Espelho das Maravilhas der erste Landstrich gewesen sein, den der portugiesische Seefahrer und Entdecker Pedro Álvares Cabral erspähte; und 1549 wurde Salvador die erste Hauptstadt Brasiliens. Den Portugiesen folgten Briten und Franzosen – unter ihrem Regime mussten die einheimischen Indios als Sklaven auf Zuckerrohrfeldern arbeiten; später brachten die Kolonialherren auch Afrikaner nach Bahia. Die fremden Mächte blieben nicht lange in der Region, hinterließen aber ein starkes Erbe: Der Dreiklang aus portugiesischer, indianischer und afrikanischer Kultur prägt noch heute das Lebensgefühl, die Architektur und die Kunst Bahias. In diesem Bundesstaat, der sich auf rund 561.000 Quadratkilometern Fläche im Nordosten Brasiliens ausdehnt, lebt man entspannt und gelassen, liebt den von Portugal beeinflussten »Tropen-Barock« sowie farbenfrohe Accessoires. Den Rahmen für den Stil Bahias bildet eine atemberaubende Natur mit rund 1.000

almost 1,000 kilometres of Atlantic coast, rivers, mangroves and dense tropical forest. The colours of nature reappear in the Brazilian flag – green stands for the country's extensive forests, yellow for its resources and blue for the sky. These stunning surroundings have inspired businessmen, architects and designers such as Ricardo Salem, Sig Bergamin and David Bastos not only to search for the best sites for their buildings but also to provide them with the finest building materials, from wood and sand to taboa fibre: here nature and architecture are often as close together as they can possibly be. This applies as much to luxurious residences as to traditional fazendas and romantic beach bungalows in the style of fishermen's huts. Whether they occupy 50 or 500 square metres, whether they were built on a generous or a modest budget, all these houses are characterised by a love of detail and of their surroundings – Bahia is not just the cradle of Brazil, but also its heart.

de kilomètres, des rivières, des mangroves et la forêt pluviale luxuriante. On retrouve ses couleurs dans le drapeau brésilien – le vert symbolise la forêt dense, le jaune les richesses du pays et le bleu son ciel. Cet environnement pittoresque a inspiré des industriels, des architectes et des designers comme Ricardo Salem, Sig Bergamin ou David Bastos. Il ne leur fournit pas seulement les plus beaux sites de construction mais aussi les meilleurs matériaux : bois, fibre de taboa, sable – ici le paysage naturel et l'architecture ne sauraient être plus proches. Cela vaut aussi bien pour les résidences de luxe que pour les fazendas traditionnelles et les bungalows de plage romantiques au faux air de cabane de pêcheur. Qu'elles aient une surface de 50 ou de 500 mètres carrés, que le budget consacré à leur construction ait été élevé ou non, toutes ces maisons ont été meublées et décorées avec un grand amour du détail et du paysage environnant. C'est que Bahia n'est pas seulement le berceau du Brésil mais aussi son cœur.

Kilometern Atlantikküste, Flüssen, Mangroven und dichtem Regenwald. Ihre Farben finden sich in der brasilianischen Flagge wieder – Grün symbolisiert den Waldreichtum des Landes, Gelb seine Schätze und Blau seinen Himmel. Diese malerische Umgebung inspiriert Unternehmer, Architekten und Designer wie Ricardo Salem, Sig Bergamin oder David Bastos nicht nur bei der Suche nach den schönsten Bauplätzen, sondern liefert ihnen vom Holz über den Sand bis hin zur Taboa-Faser auch gleich die besten Baumaterialien – Natur und Architektur kommen sich hier häufig so nahe wie nur irgend möglich. Dies gilt für mondäne Residenzen ebenso wie für traditionelle Fazendas und romantische Strandbungalows im Stil von Fischerhütten. Und ob sie 50 oder 500 Quadratmeter umfassen, mit kleinem oder großem Budget errichtet wurden: All diese Häuser sind mit Liebe zum Detail und zu ihrer Umgebung gestaltet – Bahia ist eben nicht nur die Wiege Brasiliens, sondern auch sein Herz.

"The first impression of this country is a confusing luxuriance. Everything here is stark: the sun, the light, the colours. The blue of the sky beats down more strongly here, the vegetation is a deep and saturated green, the earth dense and red..."

Stefan Zweig, *Brazil: Land of the Future*

« La première impression qu'éveille ce pays est celle d'une luxuriance déconcertante. Tout est véhément, le soleil, la lumière, les couleurs. Le bleu du ciel est plus éclatant ici, le vert profond et saturé, la terre épaisse et rouge... »

Stefan Zweig, *Brésil, terre d'avenir*

»Der erste Eindruck von diesem Lande ist der einer verwirrenden Üppigkeit. Alles ist vehement, die Sonne, das Licht, die Farben. Das Blau des Himmels schmettert hier stärker, das Grün ist tief und satt, die Erde dicht und rot ...«

Stefan Zweig, *Brasilien. Ein Land der Zukunft*

EXTERIORS

Extérieurs   Aussichten

10/11 Picture-perfect beach: Espelho das Maravilhas ("mirror of miracles") lives up to its name. *Plage de rêve : l'Espelho das Maravilhas ou Miroir des merveilles.* Bilderbuchstrand: Der Espelho das Maravilhas (Wunderspiegel) macht seinem Namen alle Ehre.

12/13 Sunshade: a simple roof of coconut straw at Espelho das Maravilhas. *Pare-soleil : un simple toit de palmes sur l'Espelho das Maravilhas.* Sonnenschutz: ein einfaches Dach aus Kokosnussstroh am Espelho das Maravilhas.

14/15 Nature: João Calazans built Fazenda Calá of concrete, brick and wooden shingles. *Nature : João Calazans a construit la Fazenda Calá en béton, briques et bardeaux.* Naturverbunden: Die Fazenda Calá erbaute João Calazans aus Beton, Ziegeln und Holzschindeln.

16/17 Simple relaxation: three posts sufficed for hanging three hammocks. *Détente : trois pieux suffisent pour fixer trois hamacs.* Einfach entspannend: Drei Pfähle genügten, um drei Hängematten zu befestigen.

18/19 Revered all over Bahia: a statue of Yemanjá, Queen of the Sea. *Vénérée à Bahia : une statue de Yemanjá, la déesse de la mer.* In ganz Bahia verehrt: eine Statue der Yemanjá, der Königin des Meeres.

20/21 A shady place to sit: a bench with rounded forms, at Fazenda Calá. *Un coin à l'ombre : un canapé maçonné aux formes arrondies dans la Fazenda Calá.* Sitzecke im Schatten: ein gemauertes Sofa mit abgerundeten Formen in der Fazenda Calá.

22/23 The 560-square-metre pool is at Casa da Península in Praia do Forte. *La piscine de 560 mètres carrés à la Casa da Península à Praia do Forte.* Der 560 Quadratmeter große Pool gehört zur Casa da Península in Praia do Forte.

24/25 Nature and architecture in harmony: Casa da Península links the exterior and interior worlds. *Harmonie : la Casa da Península marie l'intérieur et l'extérieur, la nature et l'architecture.* Harmonie von Natur und Architektur: Die Casa da Península verbindet außen und innen.

26/27 A lounge between palms and pool: in David Bastos's summer house in Praia do Forte. *Entre les palmiers et la piscine : la maison d'été de David Bastos à Praia do Forte.* Lounge zwischen Palmen und Pool: im Sommerhaus von David Bastos in Praia do Forte.

28/29 Casa de Bambu in Serra Grande, designed by Simón Vélez, is supported by bamboo. *La Casa de Bambu conçue par Simón Vélez à Serra Grande repose sur des bambous.* Die von Simón Vélez entworfene Casa de Bambu in Serra Grande steht auf Bambussäulen.

30/31 Ecology: the bamboo for the furniture is from Casa de Bambu's own land. *Écologique : les meubles ont été fabriqués avec des bambous du terrain de la Casa de Bambu.* Ökologisch: Der Bambus für die Möbel stammt vom eigenen Grundstück der Casa de Bambu.

32/33 The style of the southern states: architect Sig Bergamin's elegant summer house in Trancoso. *Style sudiste : l'élégante maison d'été de l'architecte Sig Bergamin à Trancoso.* Im Südstaatenstil: das elegante Sommerhaus des Architekten Sig Bergamin in Trancoso.

34/35 Favourite colour: Sig Bergamin chose a deep shade of blue for the tiles that line his pool. *Couleur préférée : des carreaux d'un bleu profond pour la piscine de Sig Bergamin.* Lieblingsfarbe: Sig Bergamin kleidete seinen Pool mit Kacheln in einem tiefen Blauton aus.

36/37 Shingle roof: the pergola of Ricardo Salem's house in Trancoso. *Recouverte de bardeaux : la pergola de la maison de Ricardo Salem à Trancoso.* Mit Schindeln gedeckt: die Pergola des Hauses von Ricardo Salem in Trancoso.

38/39 Teamwork: the pool furnishings were designed by Ricardo and made in Trancoso. *Travail en équipe : les meubles ont été dessinés par Ricardo Salem et fabriqués à Trancoso.* Teamwork: Die Poolmöbel wurden von Ricardo Salem entworfen und in Trancoso gefertigt.

40/41 Refreshing: jacuzzi and open-air bath of Casa do Jacaré, designed by Sig Bergamin. *Rafraîchissant : jacuzzi et terrasse à la Casa do Jacaré conçue par Sig Bergamin.* Erfrischend: Jacuzzi und Freiluftbad der von Sig Bergamin entworfenen Casa do Jacaré.

42/43 The architect, Vera Castro chose sapê fibre for the roof – like the indigenous Indians did. *Vera Castro a fait recouvrir le toit avec des fibres de sapê – à la façon des Indiens autochtones.* Vera Castro ließ das Dach mit Sapê-Fasern decken – wie es die Ureinwohner taten.

44/45 A light breeze and a wonderful ocean view can be enjoyed in the loggia designed by Vera Castro. *Dans la loggia de Vera Castro on profite d'une brise et d'une vue magnifique.* In der von Vera Castro entworfenen Loggia mit Meerblick genießt man eine leichte Brise.

46/47 Hundreds of years old: a cashew tree frames Casa 21, designed by Paulo Jacobsen. *Séculaire : Un anacardier encadre de la Casa 21 conçue par Paulo Jacobsen.* Jahrhundertealt: Ein Cashew-Baum umrahmt die Casa 21, die Paulo Jacobsen entwarf.

48/49 The power of nature: ever-present on the 40,000-square-metre grounds of Casa 21. *Puissante : La nature est omniprésente sur les 40 000 mètres carrés de la Casa 21.* Auf den 40.000 Quadratmeter großen Grundstück der Casa 21 ist die Natur allgegenwärtig.

50/51 Clay vases, spheres of natural fibre and a log bench at Casa 21 in Praia dos Coqueiros. *Jarres, boules de fibres et un tronc pour s'asseoir à la Casa 21 à Praia dos Coqueiros.* Tonvasen, Naturfaserkugeln und eine Baumstammbank in der Casa 21 in Praia dos Coqueiros.

52/53 Fabrizio Ceccarelli's Casa San Marco in Trancoso is built mainly of wood. *Signée Fabrizio Ceccarelli : La Casa San Marco à Trancoso est construite surtout en bois.* Von Fabrizio Ceccarelli erbaut: Die Casa San Marco in Trancoso ist hauptsächlich aus Holz.

54/55 Swimming beneath coconut palms: the pool of Casa San Marco. *Sous les cocotiers : La vaste piscine de la Casa San Marco.* Baden unter Kokospalmen: der Pool der Casa San Marco.

56/57 Siesta on the beach: Joana Vieira's realm is in Curuipe at Espelho das Maravilhas. *Sieste en bord de mer : Joana Vieira habite à Curuipe sur l'Espelho das Maravilhas.* Siesta am Strand: Das Reich von Joana Vieira liegt in Curuipe am Espelho das Maravilhas.

58/59 Converted: Joana Vieira's charming little house previously served as a school. *Transformée : la charmante maisonnette de Joana Vieira abritait autrefois une école.* Umgebaut: Joana Vieiras charmantes Häuschen beherbergte früher eine Schule.

60/61 A historic house: Fazenda Barra do Cahy in Prado was built more than 170 years ago. *Chargée d'histoire : la Fazenda Barra do Cahy au Prado a plus de 170 ans.* Haus mit Historie: Die Fazenda Barra do Cahy in Prado wurde vor mehr als 170 Jahren errichtet.

62/63 Blue view: Fazenda Barra do Cahy affords panoramic views of the sea and the river Cahy. *Bleu, bleu : de la Fazenda Barra do Cahy, on voit l'océan et la rivière Cahy.* Blaue Akzente: Die Fazenda Barra do Cahy eröffnet Panoramen auf das Meer und den Fluss Cahy.

64/65 Deserted: a perfect sandy beach at Nova Viçosa in southern Bahia. *Déserte : une plage de sable féerique près de Nova Viçosa au sud de Bahia.* Menschenleer: ein traumhafter Sandstrand bei Nova Viçosa im Süden Bahias.

66/67 Like the gateway to paradise: on the 1.2-square-kilometre estate Sítio Natura. *La porte du paradis : celle de la réserve naturelle de 1,2 kilomètre carré.* Wie die Pforte zum Paradies: auf dem 1,2 Quadratkilometer großen Grundstück »Sítio Natura«.

"The moon poured its light over everything; the stars seemed to glow even brighter in the sky; the sea lapped quietly…"

Jorge Amado, *Captains of the Sands*

« La lune déversait sa lumière sur tout ; les étoiles semblaient briller plus fort encore dans le ciel ; seule la mer murmurait doucement…»

Jorge Amado, *Capitaines des sables*

»Der Mond goss sein Licht über alles aus; die Sterne schienen noch stärker am Himmel zu leuchten; nur leise rauschte das Meer …«

Jorge Amado, *Herren des Strandes*

INTERIORS

Intérieurs   Einsichten

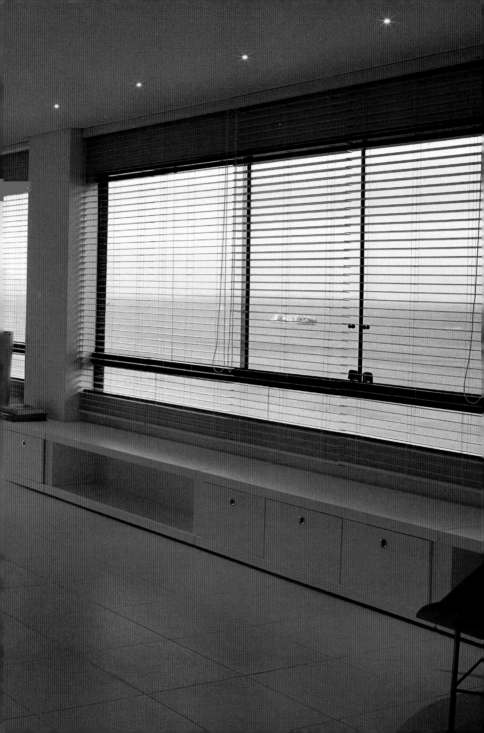

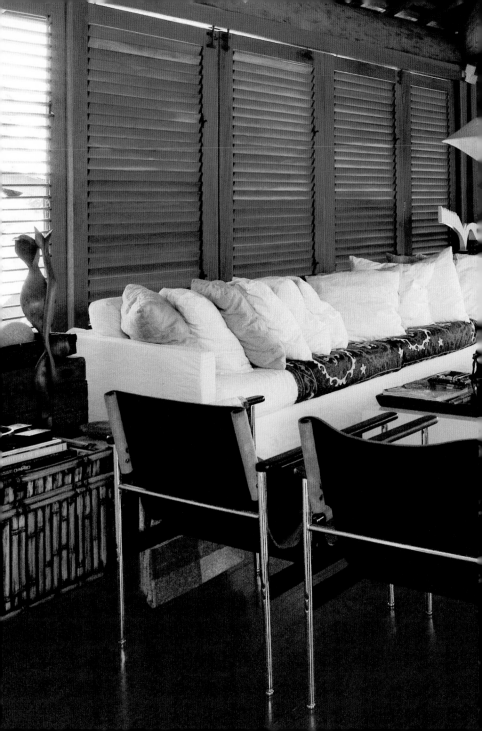

74/75 Breathtaking: Hamilton Padilha can look far out over the sea off Salvador. *Panoramique : Hamilton Padilha voit la mer devant Salvador.* Atemberaubend: Hamilton Padilha blickt weit übers Meer vor Salvador.

76/77 Golden glow: Hamilton Padilha and his architect David Bastos loved the light. *Chaleureuse : la lumière dorée a séduit Hamilton Padilha et son architecte David Bastos.* Glanzvoll: Das goldene Licht begeisterte Hamilton Padilha und seinen Architekten David Bastos.

78/79 Place of honour: a book by Helmut Newton in David Bastos's apartment in Salvador. *Place d'honneur : un album d'Helmut Newton chez David Bastos à Salvador.* Ehrenplatz: ein Helmut-Newton-Buch im Apartment von David Bastos in Salvador.

80/81 Antique furniture: the gate-leg table in Sig Bergamin's salon dates from the 19th century. *Antiquité : dans le salon de Sig Bergamin, la table Gateleg date du 19ᵉ siècle.* Antiquität: Der Gateleg-Tisch im Salon von Sig Bergamin stammt aus dem 19. Jahrhundert.

82/83 Travel souvenirs: Sig Bergamin combines furnishings and decorations from all over the world. *Souvenirs de voyage : Sig Bergamin marie les meubles et les objets du monde entier.* Reisesouvenirs: Sig Bergamin kombiniert Möbel und Wohnaccessoires aus aller Welt.

84/85 Banana plants in Vietnamese pots show the way to Sig Bergamin's dining room. *Des bananiers à l'entrée de la salle à manger de Sig Bergamin. Les pots ont été fabriqués au Vietnam.* Vor Sig Bergamins Speisezimmer stehen Bananenstauden in Töpfen aus Vietnam.

86/87 Inviting: the pergola with an open gourmet kitchen in David Bastos's house in Praia do Forte. *Engageante : la pergola et sa cuisine ouverte chez David Bastos à Praia do Forte.* Einladend: die Pergola mit offener Gourmetküche im Haus von David Bastos in Praia do Forte.

88/89 Contrasts: David Bastos combines a rustic atmosphere with the clean lines of modern furniture. *Contrastes : David Bastos marie l'ambiance rustique et les lignes modernes.* Kontraste: David Bastos verbindet rustikales Flair und geradliniges, modernes Mobiliar.

90/91 Imposing: the entrance to Casa da Peninsula, designed by Rui Córes. *Imposant : l'entrée de la Casa da Península, conçue par Rui Córes.* Imposant: Der Eingangsbereich der Casa da Península, die Rui Córes entworfen hat.

92/93 A concrete column and eucalyptus beams dominante the salon of Casa da Peninsula. *Une colonne en béton et des poutres d'eucalyptus dans le salon de la Casa da Península.* Betonsäule und Eukalyptusbalken im Salon der Casa da Península.

94/95 Vera Castro planned the wooden lounge without doors and windows. *Dans le lounge dominé par les bois, Vera Castro a renoncé aux portes et aux fenêtres.* Für die Lounge aus einheimischen Hölzern hat Vera Castro auf Türen und Fenster verzichtet.

96/97 The symmetrical living room was designed by Vera Castro. *Le living symétrique a été conçu par Vera Castro.* Das symmetrisch angelegte Wohnzimmer entwarf Vera Castro.

98/99 Living with the forest: Ricardo Salem used wood from the Atlantic rainforest. *La forêt dans le séjour : Ricardo Salem a utilisé des essences de la forêt pluviale atlantique.* Der Wald im Wohnraum: Ricardo Salem verwendet Hölzer des Atlantischen Regenwalds.

100/101 Visit from a mermaid: Ricardo Salem has furnished his house with lots of humour. *La visite de la petite sirène : Ricardo Salem a décoré sa maison avec beaucoup d'humour.* Der Besuch der Meerjungfrau: Ricardo Salem hat sein Haus humorvoll eingerichtet.

102/103 Blue glass: Ricardo Salem's decorative collection includes objects from all over the world. *Verre bleu : la collection décorative de Ricardo Salem comporte des objets du monde entier.* Blaues Glas: Die dekorative Sammlung von Ricardo Salem umfasst Objekte aus aller Welt.

104/105 In Casa 21 Paulo Jacobsen connects the lobby and bedroom by means of a broad stairway. *À la Casa 21, Paulo Jacobsen a relié le hall à la chambre à coucher par un large escalier.* In der Casa 21 verbindet Paulo Jacobsen Lobby und Schlafzimmer mit einer breiten Treppe.

106/107 Bold colours: blue foam pouffes in Casa 21 contrast with the red walls. *Il fallait oser : poufs en mousse bleue et murs rouge vermillon à la Casa 21.* Mut zur Farbe: Blaue Schaumstoffpuffs in der Casa 21 kontrastieren mit den roten Wänden.

108/109 Simplicity: in the kitchen of Fazenda Calá, cotton cloth stand in for cupboard doors. *Simplicité : des draps de coton remplacent les portes d'armoire dans la cuisine de la Fazenda Calá.* Schlichtheit: In der Küche der Fazenda Calá ersetzen Baumwolltücher die Schranktüren.

110/111 Soft cotton cushions: a built-in corner settee in Fazenda Calá. *Coussins douillets : sur un canapé de coin maçonné à la Fazenda Calá.* Mit weichen Baumwollkissen belegt: ein gemauertes Ecksofa in der Fazenda Calá.

112/113 No frills: Casa do Quadrado stands on the square of the same name in Trancoso. *Sans façon : la Casa do Quadrado, sur la place de même nom au cœur de Trancoso.* Schnörkellos: Die Casa do Quadrado steht am gleichnamigen Platz in Trancoso.

114/115 Regional materials: taboa fibre was used for the armchairs and pouffes in Casa do Quadrado. *Produit régional : fauteuil et poufs de la Casa do Quadrado en fibres de taboa.* Aus der Region: Die Sessel und die Puffs in der Casa do Quadrado sind aus Taboa-Fasern.

116/117 A touch of blue: the design of Casa do Quadrado bears the hallmark of Sig Bergamin. *Accent bleu : le design de la Casa do Quadrado est signé Sig Bergamin.* Ein Hauch von Blau: Das Design der Casa do Quadrado trägt Sig Bergamins Handschrift.

118/119 Artistically arranged: tropical leaves and crafts give the house a Brazilian feel. *Composition : végétation tropicale et réalisations artisanales – le goût brésilien entre dans la maison.* Arrangements: Tropische Blätter und Kunsthandwerk holen das Flair Brasiliens ins Haus.

120/121 A refuge: in Casa do Quadrado the owner can recover from daily life in São Paulo. *Refuge : le propriétaire de la Casa do Quadrado se repose de ses journées à São Paulo.* Refugium: In der Casa do Quadrado entspannt der Besitzer vom Alltag in São Paulo.

122/123 Sig Bergamin chose taboa fibre armchairs for the Fazenda Santo Antônio salon. *Pour le salon de la Fazenda Santo Antônio, Sig Bergamin a choisi des fauteuils en fibres de taboa.* Für den Salon der Fazenda Santo Antônio wählte Sig Bergamin Sessel aus Taboa-Fasern.

124/125 Nizan Guanaes and his wife often entertain friends in Fazenda Santo Antônio. *Nizan Guanaes et son épouse régalent souvent leurs amis à la Fazenda Santo Antônio.* Nizan Guanaes und seine Frau bewirten in der Fazenda Santo Antônio häufig Freunde.

126/127 A flowered carpet made from scraps of fabric: Isabel Duprat's little summer house in Curuipe. *Fleuri': un tapis en restes de tissu dans la petite maison d'été d'Isabel Duprat à Curuipe.* Ein Blumenteppich aus Stoffresten: im kleinen Sommerhaus von Isabel Duprat in Curuipe.

128/129 A unique item: the sofa covered in a flower pattern was made in Trancoso for Isabel Duprat. *Unique : Isabel Duprat a fait fabriquer à Trancoso le canapé recouvert d'une housse fleurie.* Einzelstück: Das Blumenmuster-Sofa ließ Isabel Duprat in Trancoso herstellen.

130/131 Isabel Duprat's bedroom with a mosquito net and a sloping roof of coconut fibre. *La chambre à coucher d'Isabel Duprat avec sa moustiquaire et son plafond habillé de fibres de coco.* Der Schlafraum von Isabel Duprat mit Moskitonetz und Dachgiebel aus Kokosfasern.

132/133 Joana Vieira mixes items of Brazilian popular culture with white lace covers. *Joana Vieira marie des nappes en dentelle blanche à des accessoires populaires brésiliens.* Joana Vieira mischt brasilianische Volkskultur mit weißen Spitzendecken.

134/135 Pots, plates and cutlery are always at hand in Joana Vieira's kitchen. *Dans la cuisine, Joana Vieira a toujours les casseroles, la vaisselle et les couverts sous la main.* In Joana Vieiras Küche sind Töpfe, Teller und Besteck immer zur Hand.

136/137 Peace and contemplation: Joana Vieira has a private altar behind her bed. *Contemplative : Joana Vieira dispose d'un autel particulier derrière son lit.* Ruhe und Besinnung: Hinter dem Bett von Joana Vieira verbirgt sich ein privater Altar.

138/139 The atmosphere is bright in Nana Salles and Flávio Marelim's home in Ponta do Camarão. *Accents lumineux chez Nana Salles et Flávio Marelim à Ponta do Camarão.* Fröhliche Akzente bei Nana Salles und Flávio Marelim in Ponta do Camarão.

140/141 The dining table is the focal point of this wooden house, which is just 75 square metres in size. *La table est le point de mire dans la maison en bois de 75 mètres carrés.* Der Esstisch ist Mittelpunkt des nur 75 Quadratmeter großen Holzhauses.

142/143 Pleasant surroundings: the cosy bedroom of Nana Salles and Flávio Marelim. *Douceur : la chambre à coucher confortable de Nana Salles et Flávio Marelim.* Angenehmes Ambiente: im gemütlichen Schlafzimmer von Nana Salles und Flávio Marelim.

144/145 The style of local fishermen's houses: the home of Carla and Tuca Reinés in Vila do Outeiro. *Style cabane de pêcheur: le foyer de Carla et Tuca Reinés à Vila do Outeiro.* Im Stil einheimischer Fischerhäuser: das Heim von Carla und Tuca Reinés in Vila do Outeiro.

146/147 Their own ideas: Tuca Reinés designed the house, his wife, Carla, the clean lines of the interior. *Duo : Tuca Reinés a conçu la maison, son épouse Carla le sobre décor intérieur.* Eigene Ideen: Tuca Reinés entwarf das Haus, seine Frau Carla das geradlinige Interieur.

148/149 Lots of space to play: a child's room in the home of Georgia and Eric Reinés. *Ludique : la chambre des enfants, Georgia et Eric Reinés.* Viel Platz zum Spielen: im Kinderzimmer von Georgia und Eric Reinés.

"He raised his eyes to the pastel-coloured orchids, which looked as if they had just landed on the branches of the larger trees, light and fragile as paper birds..."

João Ubaldo Ribeiro, *An Invincible Memory*

« Il leva les yeux vers les orchidées couleur pastel, qui avaient l'air de s'être posées à l'instant sur les branches des plus grands arbres, légères et fragiles comme des oiseaux en papier... »

João Ubaldo Ribeiro, *Vive le peuple brésilien*

»Er hob den Blick zu den pastellfarbenen Orchideen, die aussahen, als hätten sie sich gerade auf den Ästen der größeren Bäume niedergelassen, leicht und fragil wie Papiervögel ...«

João Ubaldo Ribeiro, *Brasilien, Brasilien*

DETAILS

Détails   Details

156 A map of South America from the late 18th or early 19th century. *Carte de l'Amérique du Sud datant de la fin du 18ᵉ début du 19ᵉ siècle. Die Südamerikakarte stammt vom Ende des 18., Anfang des 19. Jahrhunderts.*

158 National drink: cachaça is also known as aguardente (fire water). *Boisson nationale : la cachaça, l'eau de vie de canne à sucre, aussi appelée aguardente (eau de feu). Nationalgetränk: Der Cachaça wird auch Aguardente (Feuerwasser) genannt.*

159 Fresh limes: an essential part of Brazilian caipirinha. *Incontournables : pas de caipirinha sans citrons verts. Frische Limetten: Sie gehören in jede brasilianische Caipirinha.*

160 A small chapel: in the grounds of Fazenda Barra do Cahy. *Accueillante : une petite chapelle à la Fazenda Barra do Cahy. Eine kleine Kapelle: auf dem Grundstück der Fazenda Barra do Cahy.*

162 A speciality: fresh sea anemones are grilled over the hot coals. *Spécialité : des oursins sont grillés sur les braises. Spezialität: Über den glühenden Kohlen werden frische Seeigel gegrillt.*

163 Maritime decoration: Seafood is served on dishes to match. *Décor maritime : fruits de mer servis sur des assiettes assorties. Maritimes Dekor: mediterrane Küche auf passendem Geschirr.*

165 The flag: colours stand for the extensive forests, resources and sky of Brazil. *Le drapeau : les couleurs évoquent la forêt, les richesses et le ciel du Brésil. Die Flagge: Die Farben stehen für Waldreichtum, Schätze und den Himmel Brasiliens.*

166 Brazilian heart: a keyring made from scraps of material. *Un cœur pour le Brésil : le porte-clés est fait de restes de tissu. Ein Herz für Brasilien: Der Schlüsselanhänger wurde aus Stoffresten hergestellt.*

167 For the Queen of the Sea: Joana Vieira designed this altar to Yemanjá. *Pour la déesse de l'eau : Joana Vieira a créé l'autel à Yemanjá. Für die Königin des Meeres: Den Yemanjá-Altar hat Joana Vieira gestaltet.*

168 Integrated into nature: the pergola of Casa 21 in Praia dos Coqueiros. *Intégrée dans le paysage : la vaste pergola de la Casa 21 à Praia dos Coqueiros. Eins mit der Natur: die weitläufige Pergola der Casa 21 in Praia dos Coqueiros.*

170 A practical use: the plaster figures of saints Cosmas and Damian serve as a lamp. *Pratique : les saints en plâtre Cosme et Damien servent de lampe. Praktisch: die Gipsfiguren der Heiligen Kosmas und Damian als Lampe.*

171 Yemanjá, Queen of the Sea, watches over the beach of Espelho das Maravilhas. *Yemanjá, la reine des eaux, regarde la plage Espelho das Maravilhas. Die Meereskönigin Yemanjá überblickt den Strand Espelho das Maravilhas.*

173 A new function: in Fazenda Calá a tin bucket serves as a shower. *Recyclage : à la Fazenda Calá, un seau en tôle sert de douche. Neue Funktion: In der Fazenda Calá dient ein ehemaliger Blecheimer als Dusche.*

174 The airy bathroom with rain-jet showers by Nana Salles and Flávio Marelim. *La salle de bains claire avec sa douche-pluie chez Nana Salles et Flávio Marelim.* Das luftige Bad mit Regenduschen bei Nana Salles und Flávio Marelim.

175 Plaster decoration: fish and sea stars adorn the toilet of Fazenda Calá. *En plâtre : étoiles de mer et poissons ornent l'accès aux toilettes de la Fazenda Calá.* Aus Gips geformt: Fische und Seesterne über der Toilettentür der Fazenda Calá.

176 Sea-blue: the bathroom of Fazenda Santo Antônio on Itapororoca beach. *Bleu azur : la salle de bains de la Fazenda Santo Antônio sur la plage d'Itapororoca.* Meerblau: im Bad der Fazenda Santo Antônio am Itapororoca-Strand.

178 Delicate: a key with feathers from native birds, in Casa do Quadrado. *Filigrane : une clé ornée des plumes d'oiseaux de la région à la Casa do Quadrado.* Filigran: ein mit heimischen Federn geschmückter Schlüssel in der Casa do Quadrado.

179 "The woodpecker's house": wood was Ricardo Salem's main material. *« La maison du pic » : Ricardo Salem a surtout utilisé du bois.* »Haus des Spechts«: Ricardo Salem nutzte hauptsächlich Holz.

181 All lined up: the straw pouffes on the terrace of Casa 21. *En rangs serrés : les poufs en paille sur la terrasse de la Casa 21.* In Reih und Glied: die Strohpuffs auf einer Terrasse der Casa 21.

182 No metal: even hinges are made of wood in many Bahia houses. *Métal banni : dans de nombreuses maisons de Bahia, même les charnières sont en bois.* Kein Metall: Selbst Scharniere sind in vielen Häusern Bahias aus Holz.

183 Dense vegetation: a view of the garden of Casa San Marco through the blinds. *Verdure : le jardin de la Casa San Marco vu à travers les jalousies.* Dichtes Grün: Durch Jalousien blickt man in den Garten der Casa San Marco.

184 Lunch beneath cashew trees: the garden of Casa 21 is a natural paradise. *Sous les anacardiers : déjeuner dans le jardin sauvage de la Casa 21.* Mittagessen unter knorrigen Cashew-Bäumen: Im naturbelassenen Garten der Casa 21.

186 The hall has a symmetrical look, with partitions and lamps. *Le corridor est symétrique avec des murs écrans espacés et des luminaires.* Der Flur wirkt mit Halbwänden und den Leuchten symetrisch. Architect: Vera Castro

187 Even the accessories take up the colours of the surroundings. *On retrouve les couleurs de l'environnement dans les accessoires.* Selbst die Accessoires greifen die Farben der Umgebung wieder auf. Architect: Vera Castro

189 Trompe-l'œil painting: artwork in Casa do Picchio by Pascal Rochette. *Trompe-l'œil : cette œuvre dans la Casa do Picchio est signée Pascal Rochette.* Trompe-l'œil-Malerei: ein Kunstwerk in der Casa do Picchio von Pascal Rochette.

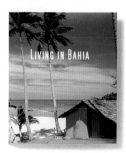

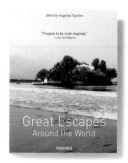

Living in Bahia
Ed. Angelika Taschen / Photos:
Tuca Reinés / Texts: Mônica Lima /
Hardcover, 200 pp. / € 19.99 /
$ 29.99 / £ 16.99 / ¥ 3.900

**Great Escapes Around
the World**
Ed. Angelika Taschen
Hardcover, 720 pp. / € 39.99 /
$ 59.99 / £ 29.99 / ¥ 7.900

**Great Escapes Around
the World. Vol. 2**
Ed. Angelika Taschen
Hardcover, 672 pp. / € 39.99 /
$ 59.99 / £ 29.99 / ¥ 7.900

"Get inspired to create a laid-back style with a relaxed Brazilian twist in TASCHEN's *Living in Bahia*." —*Flare*, Los Angeles, on *Living in Bahia*

"Buy them all and add some pleasure to your life."

60s Fashion
Ed. Jim Heimann

70s Fashion
Ed. Jim Heimann

African Style
Ed. Angelika Taschen

Alchemy & Mysticism
Alexander Roob

Architecture Now!
Ed. Philip Jodidio

Art Now
Eds. Burkhard Riemschneider,
Uta Grosenick

Atget's Paris
Ed. Hans Christian Adam

Bamboo Style
Ed. Angelika Taschen

**Barcelona,
Restaurants & More**
Ed. Angelika Taschen

**Barcelona,
Shops & More**
Ed. Angelika Taschen

Ingrid Bergman
Ed. Paul Duncan, Scott Eyman

Berlin Style
Ed. Angelika Taschen

Humphrey Bogart
Ed. Paul Duncan, James Ursini

Marlon Brando
Ed. Paul Duncan, F.X. Feeney

Brussels Style
Ed. Angelika Taschen

Cars of the 70s
Ed. Jim Heimann, Tony Thacker

Charlie Chaplin
Ed. Paul Duncan,
David Robinson

China Style
Ed. Angelika Taschen

Christmas
Ed. Jim Heimann, Steven Heller

James Dean
Ed. Paul Duncan, F.X. Feeney

Design Handbook
Charlotte & Peter Fiell

Design for the 21ˢᵗ Century
Eds. Charlotte & Peter Fiell

Design of the 20ᵗʰ Century
Eds. Charlotte & Peter Fiell

Devils
Gilles Néret

Marlene Dietrich
Ed. Paul Duncan, James Ursini

Robert Doisneau
Jean-Claude Gautrand

East German Design
Ralf Ulrich/Photos: Ernst Hedler

Clint Eastwood
Ed. Paul Duncan, Douglas
Keesey

Egypt Style
Ed. Angelika Taschen

Encyclopaedia Anatomica
Ed. Museo La Specola Florence

M.C. Escher

Fashion
Ed. The Kyoto Costume Institute

Fashion Now!
Eds. Terry Jones, Susie Rushton

Fruit
Ed. George Brookshaw,
Uta Pellgrü-Gagel

Greta Garbo
Ed. Paul Duncan, David
Robinson

HR Giger
HR Giger

Grand Tour
Harry Seidler

Cary Grant
Ed. Paul Duncan, F.X. Feeney

Graphic Design
Eds. Charlotte & Peter Fiell

Greece Style
Ed. Angelika Taschen

Halloween
Ed. Jim Heimann, Steven Heller

Havana Style
Ed. Angelika Taschen

Audrey Hepburn
Ed. Paul Duncan, F.X. Feeney

Katharine Hepburn
Ed. Paul Duncan, Alain Silver

Homo Art
Gilles Néret

Hot Rods
Ed. Coco Shinomiya, Tony
Thacker

Grace Kelly
Ed. Paul Duncan, Glenn Hopp

London, Restaurants & More
Ed. Angelika Taschen

London, Shops & More
Ed. Angelika Taschen

London Style
Ed. Angelika Taschen

Marx Brothers
Ed. Paul Duncan, Douglas
Keesey

Steve McQueen
Ed. Paul Duncan, Alain Silver

Mexico Style
Ed. Angelika Taschen

Miami Style
Ed. Angelika Taschen

Minimal Style
Ed. Angelika Taschen

Marilyn Monroe
Ed. Paul Duncan, F.X. Feeney

Morocco Style
Ed. Angelika Taschen

New York Style
Ed. Angelika Taschen

Paris Style
Ed. Angelika Taschen

Penguin
Frans Lanting

Pierre et Gilles
Eric Troncy

Provence Style
Ed. Angelika Taschen

Safari Style
Ed. Angelika Taschen

Seaside Style
Ed. Angelika Taschen

Signs
Ed. Julius Wiedeman

South African Style
Ed. Angelika Taschen

Starck
Philippe Starck

Surfing
Ed. Jim Heimann

Sweden Style
Ed. Angelika Taschen

Tattoos
Ed. Henk Schiffmacher

Tokyo Style
Ed. Angelika Taschen

Tuscany Style
Ed. Angelika Taschen

Valentines
Ed. Jim Heimann, Steven Heller

Web Design: Best Studios
Ed. Julius Wiedemann

Web Design: Best Studios 2
Ed. Julius Wiedemann

Web Design: E-Commerce
Ed. Julius Wiedemann

Web Design: Flash Sites
Ed. Julius Wiedemann

**Web Design: Interactive &
Games**
Ed. Julius Wiedemann

Web Design: Music Sites
Ed. Julius Wiedemann

Web Design: Video Sites
Ed. Julius Wiedemann

Web Design: Portfolios
Ed. Julius Wiedemann

Orson Welles
Ed. Paul Duncan, F.X. Feeney

Women Artists 20ᵗʰ & 21ˢᵗ Cent.
Ed. Uta Grosenick

ICONS